Profit and Expense Control

Donald N. Lombardi

Profit and Expense Control

Table of Contents

Profit and Expense Control

Linking People to Profit

Successful management makes successful organizations. The intelligent management of people and profit has become the critical role of business today. The planning, organizing, and controlling of management work is vital to meeting business objectives. **As the owner and/or manager of a business you are probably aware of areas in which you could operate more profitably and more efficiently**. But when you have a business to run, it is hard enough to cope with today, let alone plan for tomorrow and have fun doing it.

We are here to help you "separate the forest from the trees". For the past twenty years we have worked with thousands of small business owners and have developed the most essential business operating procedures for success of their enterprises. **These procedures have been field tested and proven to be effective in most of our consulting assignments.**

You can use these operating procedures in multiple departments of your company immediately, and easily edit and customize them in Microsoft Word to fit your company needs.

Many organizations of all industry types and sizes have discovered the remarkable differences these operating procedures can make in achieving the following:

- A more disciplined approach to profit and growth.
- A more realistic balance between long and short term objectives.
- A better capacity for dealing with change.
- A better utilization of organizational resources; human, material and financial.
- A stronger management team.
- A more meaningful performance and control system.

Owner/Operators can save countless hours of research, planning, and development time by using prewritten policies and procedures for accounting, people management and more.

We have personally field tested and proven these operating policies and procedures to be successful in most client situations. They are now documented here and made part of **Business Operating Procedures.**

Profit and Expense Control

Cash Flow Forecast

1.0 INTRODUCTION

1.1 The purpose of this Standard Procedure is to establish and define a new methodology and format for use by the company in projecting its Weekly Cash Position.

1.2 The main objective of preparing such a projection within the company is to determine deficiencies or excesses in Cash Flow from what is necessary to operate the business.

1.3 If deficiencies are revealed in the Cash Flow, financial plans must be altered to provide more cash or reduce expenses. In cases where excess cash is revealed it might indicate excessive borrowing or idle money that can be put to work or be used to pay down debt, A/P accounts, etc. The primary objective is for the company to become "more" pro-active, thus utilizing a Cash Flow Forecasting Program.

1.4 The secondary objective is to ensure "Financial Adherence" to the company's Annual Operating Plan. Due to the fact that the company is going to develop an Annual Operating Plan, it is important that the Cash Flow be representative of the Plan.

2.0 ADVANTAGES

2.1 Like any planning, the preparation and maintenance of a Cash Flow Projection requires some time and effort. In nearly all cases, the advantage of doing the forecast far outweighs the effort required by the company.

2.2 The Six Week Cash Flow developed for the company enables evaluation of the implications of purchasing decisions six (6) weeks out, before expenditures are committed that may subsequently be difficult to handle with the current Cash Flow.

2.3 This forecasting technique sharpens your awareness of deadlines such as those for billing, payroll, payables or tax obligations.

Profit and Expense Control

Cash Flow Forecast

2.4 As a control device, the Six Week Cash Flow Forecast can provide checkpoints to compare against actual results. Deviation from expected results could mean that plans are not realistic and may need revision. The deviations signal the need for timely management attention.

2.5 Essentially the Cash Flow Forecast is a tabulation of the company's plans, expressed in terms of their impact on incoming and outgoing dollar flow.

2.6 The main objective of a Six Week Cash Flow Forecast is to predict when and in what quantities the dollars will come into and go out of the company.

3.0 BACKGROUND

3.1 Assembling background data will be facilitated by the use of data available from the budgeting process and/or the sales forecast.

3.2 Since the budget process and reporting of variances from the budget are totally dependent upon careful planning, it is possible to maintain Cash Flow Forecasting on a more accurate basis than for companies who do not budget at all.

3.3 The company will need the following data before making the Cash Flow Forecast:

  3.3.1 Accounts Payable Aging: Existing Payables must be accommodated at the time the Cash Flow Forecast is made. This is done by preparing an aging of payables and making Management decisions regarding payment of each.

  3.3.2 Other Disbursements: Existing long or short-term debt must be retired as agreed upon. Other obligations such as taxes and insurance must be paid. There may be a plan for capital expenditures. All non-operating statement pay-outs are to be listed according to their due dates and amounts.

Profit and Expense Control

Cash Flow Forecast

The background is easily connected to the Cash Flow Forecast by following the procedure below.   Maintaining the currency of the information is routine and will facilitate the formulation of future Cash Flow Forecasts.

4.0   PROCEDURE

4.1   Cash Flow Forecast is most precise over the short term and become less precise as they are pushed further into the future. For this reason, the forecast suggested here covers the coming six (6) weeks and is updated weekly, with a week added and one dropped.

4.2   The forecast is done on a computer spreadsheet such as Microsoft Excel. The Cash Flow Forecast is kept up to date by filling in the actual result at the end of the week, altering the projection as necessary, and adding a week in the projection as the first week ends.

4.3   Monday morning, the previous week's actual expenditures should be entered into the actual column. Be sure to include any checks written for which there was no estimate. **IMPORTANT: _The ending cash available should agree with the check register._**

4.4   This result should be printed and on the owner's desk by a specific time (such as 10:00 A.M.)

4.5   After printing, the form should be updated with all information being moved ahead to the next week.

4.6   Enter the new week ending date.

4.7   Enter the new beginning bank balance.

4.8   Enter the new forecast for the sixth week.

Profit and Expense Control

Cash Flow Forecast

5.0 ADJUSTMENTS

5.1 Unless the forecast shows relatively even and healthy cash surplus for each period some adjustments will have to be made to overcome predicted shortages.

5.2 Certain payments may have to be deferred. Refer to Accounts Payable aging, the sales related expenses and the operating expenses to determine if this is possible. If so, make the necessary adjustments.

5.3 Adjust payment for capital expenditure to match Cash Flow.

Profit and Expense Control

Cash Flow Forecast

Six Week Cash Flow Forecast

Company Name

Fill in Dates for:	1st Week Ending Saturday -		2nd Week Ending Saturday -
Revenues	**Estimated**	**Actual**	**Estimated**
Beginning Balance	0	0	0
Total Revenues	0	0	0
Expenses			
Total Expenses	0	0	0
Ending Cash Balance	0	0	0

Profit and Expense Control

Profit Plan Preparation

1.0 INTRODUCTION

1.1 The purpose of this procedure is to describe the development of the Annual Operating Profit Plan for the company.

1.2 The development of the annual Profit Plan, or Budget, is the first major step in controlling the expenses of the company. From the annual Profit Plan it is then possible to develop monthly Profit Plan guidelines.

2.0 CONCEPT

2.1 Any operating Profit Plan must be realistic and attainable. Merely guessing at hoped for sales and entering best guess numbers into expense categories will not necessarily result in obtaining planned profit.

2.2 The annual Profit Plan will be based primarily on historic data of the company, taken from the financial statements, in conjunction with assessment of charges in the period for which the Profit Plan is being prepared.

2.3 It is recommended that an Income and Expense Review be used to determine the benchmark for the line item expenses, using the following criteria:

2.3.1 Variable expenses are determined as a percent of sales. These are the costs of producing sales and should vary in direct proportion to the revenue. The Income and Expense Review will show the most favorable performance attained in the past three years.

2.3.2 The Income and Expense Review will also show the best performance in the period for fixed cost dollars. These figures should remain constant regardless of the revenue volume. Management decisions should be the determining factor for the fixed costs.

Profit and Expense Control

Profit Plan Preparation

Some expense line items require Zero Based budgeting, determining the goal by analyzing the actual amount that will be required. All components of a Zero Based budget item must be justified. Examples of expenses falling into this category may be Rent, Administrative Salaries, Insurance, etc.

2.4 The entire Profit Plan must be reviewed and the historical percentages and dollar amounts modified, based on the judgment of management.

3.0 PREPARING THE ANNUAL PROFIT PLAN

3.1 For easy translation, the Profit Plan should be prepared using the same format as the company Income Statements.

3.2 Once the annual revenue goal is established, we then break down the revenue categories based on the estimated percentage each should contribute.

3.3 The next area to be addressed will be the profit goal.

3.4 The Variable Expenses will be determined by the predetermined percent to total revenue.

3.5 The Fixed Expenses will be entered as a dollar amount, based on management decision, either from historic figures or zero based budgeting.

3.6 The Cost of Sales Expenses will be subtracted from Total Income to determine Gross Margin.

3.7 Overhead Expenses are then totaled and subtracted from the Gross Margin and the Net Operating Income derived. If the Net Operating Income figure does not meet or exceed the profit goal, each line item must be reviewed and adjustments made to hit the goal.

Profit and Expense Control

Profit Plan Preparation

4.0 MONTHLY PROFIT PLAN GUIDELINES

4.1 In order to establish monthly guidelines in a company that is not drastically affected by seasonality, a flex Budget will be used.

5.0 BUDGETARY PROCESS

5.1 This budget should be updated in November for the next fiscal year.

5.2 Profit Plan worksheets should be distributed to key personnel. This will allow them to provide their input on each line item for which they are responsible.

5.3 A follow-up meeting should be held two weeks after the initial meeting to review the individual Profit Plan projections. Each manager will be called upon to justify their budget figures.

5.4 Once the Profit plan figures are reviewed, compiled and agreed upon, they will be entered into the Profit Plan format, for review at a subsequent meeting.

5.5 The next meeting to be held within two weeks will be held for the purpose of reviewing the Profit Plan results. If the figures do not produce the desired profit potential, trimming individual line items must be addressed.

5.6 The meetings must be scheduled to ensure completion of the Profit Plan for preliminary Ownership approval by December 1st, to allow final approval by December 15th.

Profit and Expense Control

Profit Plan Preparation

6.0 BUDGETING FOR A PROFIT

6.1 Desired profit should be predetermined and included in the Profit Plan as the primary item of expense.

6.2 If the budget profit figure is below the goal desired, examine ways to enhance the revenue figures, reduce the expenses, or both.

7.0 DATA ENTRY

7.1 The budget worksheet (see attachment) is set up with the same order as a Profit and Loss Statement, with the sub accounts in italics.

7.2 All Cost of Goods Sold line items are established by multiplying the Total Income amount by the desired percent to revenue figure. The Account headers that have reporting sub accounts will automatically total, such as Advertising, Contract Labor, etc.

7.3 The G&A Expenses will be entered as dollar amounts and the % to revenue figures will automatically calculate. Again the account headers will total from the sub account entries.

7.4 The Break Even and Overhead Allocation figures are all formulas taken from figures in the body of the budget, and will automatically change if any line items in the budget are changed.

Profit and Expense Control

Profit Plan Preparation

8.0 SUMMARY

8.1   Once the Profit Plan is completed, it must be reviewed at least once each month to determine the company's compliance with the figures and react accordingly. These reviews (Monthly Variance Reports) will also alert us to flaws in the budgetary process or accounting procedures.

8.2   Management cannot sit back and expect the planned profit to accrue because a Profit Plan has been developed. Concentrate on the attainment of the revenue goal and maintaining the expenses at or below the Profit Plan levels. Once the Profit Plan has been developed, it is the responsibility of management to **Make it happen!**

Profit and Expense Control

Flexible Budget

1.0   **BUDGET WORKSHEET (Software may be downloaded at: http://shop.businessoperatingprocedures.com).**

1.1   The Budget Worksheet is on an Excel Spread Sheet which has been loaded into this Microsoft Word Document. In order to use the "Worksheet" you will need to remove it from the Word Doc and Convert it to a Range on a blank Excel Spread sheet:

1.1.1   Click twice anywhere on the Budget Worksheet.

1.1.2   "Tools" will appear above the "Design" label.

1.1.3   Click on "Tools" and "Convert to Range" will appear in the Tool Box.

1.1.4   Click on "Convert to Range" and with your mouse scan over the full range of the worksheet that you wish to copy; i.e.: "A1 to K44".

1.1.5   Use your mouse to "Copy" and then proceed to "Paste" on a new Excel Spreadsheet.

Property				
Total Expense				
Operating Profit (Loss)				

Profit and Expense Control

Breakeven Analysis

1.0 INTRODUCTION

1.0 The purpose of this procedure is to describe the method of calculating Breakeven Points and using Breakeven Analysis for decision making.

1.1 Breakeven Analysis is a useful financial tool for strategic (long range) business planning. It allows determination of projected profit or loss and the Breakeven point.

1.2 Breakeven Analysis can help identify and analyze the anticipated effect of financial action before they are taken.

1.3 The Breakeven Point identifies the amount of safety net between projected volume and incurring a loss, if expenses are controlled.

2.0 DEFINITION OF BREAKEVEN

2.0 Breakeven Analysis is a management tool which uses the most correct financial information to calculate the level of operation at which a business "breaks even". The Breakeven point shows the point at which a company has neither lost nor made a profit.

2.1 The Breakeven Point is that level of Sales at which all expenses, fixed and variable are covered and the company begins to make a profit.

3.0 DEFINING BREAKEVEN EXPENSE ELEMENTS

3.0 Fixed Expenses: The expenses of running the business. These expenses are stable and unchanging over a wide range of operating levels. They normally do not change with the level of sales activity.

Profit and Expense Control

Breakeven Analysis

3.1   They are expenses of doing business. Good examples of fixed expenses are Utilities, Rent, and Administrative Payroll. These expenses remain stable regardless of sales volume.

3.2   Variable Expense: The expenses of producing the company revenues. These expenses should always vary directly with the level of business activity (Revenue).

3.3   Breakeven Point: The point at which revenue equals direct expenses and fixed expenses, and net profit equals zero.

4.0   COMPUTING THE BREAKEVEN POINT

4.0   To obtain base statistics for the computation of Breakeven, the most recent Profit and Loss Statement or the budget projections for the coming year should be used and analyzed.

4.1   The actual or the derived statistics of the business must be aligned or accumulated according to their particular expense category; i.e.: fixed or variable. Then, total each expense category.

4.2   The following formula will be used to calculate the Breakeven Point:

$$\text{Breakeven Point}: \quad BE = \frac{\text{Total Fixed Expenses}}{1.0 \quad - \text{Total Direct Expenses/Revenue}}$$

4.3   Example: Using the next twelve months budget figures:

Total Revenue ®	$1,659,780
Total Fixed (FE)	408,925
Total Variable (VE)	615,280
Total Fixed and Variable	1,024,205
Net Income	635,575

Profit and Expense Control

Breakeven Analysis

$$BE = \frac{FE}{1.0-VE/R} = \frac{408{,}925}{1.0 - .3707} = \frac{408{,}925}{.6293} = \mathbf{\$649{,}809}$$

Based on the Operating Budget, the Breakeven Point is $649,809 for the year or $54,151 per month.

5.0 USING BREAKEVEN ANALYSIS

5.0 Addition of either Fixed or Variable Expense will have a very significant effect on the Breakeven, and decisions to increase these expenses must be based on the following three factors:

5.0.1 Effect on the Net Income: the annual expense incurred must be factored into the Operating Budget and the bottom line profitability assessed. If the company profit goals cannot be attained, the decision may not be sound.

5.0.2 Effect on Cash Flow: the monthly outlay of cash must be factored in the cash flow forecast and the result assessed. If this decision reduces that Ending Cash Balance below the acceptable level the decision may not be sound.

5.0.3 Effect on Breakeven Point: this is the most often overlooked factor. If the effect on the Breakeven Point reduces the safety net below a comfortable level, the decision may not be sound.

5.0.4 Example #1: If an administrative employee is added at an annual cost of $35,000 this will have the following impact:

Total Revenue ®	$1,659,780
Total Fixed Expense (FE) + 35,000	443,925
Total Variable Expense (VE)	615,280
Total Fixed and Variable	1,059,205
Net Income	600,575

Profit and Expense Control

Breakeven Analysis

$$BE = \underline{\quad FE \quad} = \underline{\quad 443{,}925 \quad} = \underline{\quad 443{,}925 \quad} = \mathbf{705{,}428}$$
$$ \quad 1.0\text{-VE/R} \qquad 1.0\text{ -}.3707 \qquad .6293$$

The decision had a negative effect on Net Income of $35,000 but the effect on the breakeven point is an increase of $55,618 or $4,635 per month.

5.1 This type of calculation may be applied to all major management decisions and effect analyzed. If the "Safety Net" provided by the Breakeven point becomes too thin for comfort, the decision should be entered into with **extreme caution.**

6.0 REVENUE INCREASE CALCULATION

6.0 When considering an increase in the expense structure, either direct expense percentage or overhead dollars, it is important to understand the how much additional revenue will be required to maintain the same profit dollars.

6.0.1 For example: if an expenditure has been approved that adds $40,000 to the current expense structure, the addition revenue necessary to replace the profit deterioration is calculated as follows:

- Additional Revenue = Expense Increase/Net Profit %

$104,466 = 40,000/.3829

This additional revenue will replace the $40,000 on the bottom line, but will reduce the net profit percentage, because the revenue has gone up but the net profit has not.

Profit and Expense Control

Variance Report

1.0 INTRODUCTION

1.1 This procedure explains the preparation and analysis of the Monthly Variance Report to ensure control of expenses.

1.2 The difference between the actual expenses and the Monthly Projected Budget for each expense is calculated as the Variance. Negative (unfavorable) variances are identified and corrective action taken to control a problem quickly. The ultimate purpose of this effort is to achieve, if not surpass, the desired operating profit.

1.3 The Variance Report must be designed to allow for accurate tracking of variable expenses as revenue productivity fluctuates.

2.0 PURPOSE

2.1 The Variance Report is designed as a report card to indicate how well the company is controlling expenses. In addition, Variance Reports will also indicate when there are errors in the accounting process, as well as flaws in the budget.

2.2 The Variance will be generated on a monthly basis as soon as the financial statements are available. It is important that the in house accounting system be maintained daily to provide accurate data within the first four days following the close of each month.

3.0 FORMAT

3.1 The Variance Report is set up in the Financials workbook on Excel and can be easily updated as soon as the Profit and Loss Statement is available each month.

Profit and Expense Control

Variance Report

3.2   The report has the following columns:

    3.2.1   Monthly Budget: These figures can be copied and pasted directly from the 100% column on the flex budget worksheet.

    3.2.2   Actual: These figures will come directly from the monthly Profit and Loss Statement, and will be keyed in the appropriate revenue and expense categories in the Actual column. Sub-account figures will be keyed in and Account Headers will automatically calculate.

    3.2.3   Re-budget Standard: This column reflects the adjustment that must be made to variable expenses as revenues fluctuate from the original budget. The Re-budget Factor is calculated by dividing the actual revenue total by the budgeted revenue total. The re-budget factor is then applied to each of the variable expenses to reflect the appropriate adjustments.

    3.2.4a   Variance (Expense): Subtract the Actual column from the Re-budget Standard column to obtain the dollar variance for expenses. Negative expense variances are unfavorable.

    3.2.4b   Variance (Gross Margin, Net Ordinary Income): Subtract the Re-budget Standard figure from the Actual figure. Negative revenue end results variances are unfavorable.

    3.2.5   Variance Percent: The percentage of variance to the budget amount. Divide the variance amount by the original budget amount.

    3.2.6   Notes: This column will be used by management to make notations to explain the variances and the corrective action that will be taken.

Profit and Expense Control

Variance Report

4.0 ANALYSIS AND ACTION

4.1 The primary analysis is to determine the cause of the variances, especially unfavorable variance. Causes of the variances must be justified, not rationalized.

4.2 When unfavorable variances occur, it is imperative that management take corrective action, to prevent the situation from recurring and to try to recover the loss.

4.3 If a positive variance is significant, you must also determine the cause. If there were extenuating circumstances for the variances, it is important that these be understood.

4.4 When reviewing the Variance Report on a monthly basis it is important to make notes to explain the variances, allowing you to refer back in subsequent months to review and analyze the corrective action.

4.5 Variance Report should be kept in a binder with the most current report to the front. This will provide a useful reference to prior problems or corrective action.

5.0 CONCLUSION

5.1 The budget is to provide a foundation to manage by Plan. People can generally make happen what they plan, if communication and follow up occur.

5.2 The Variance Report pinpoints exceptions to the plan, so corrective action can be taken. This allows management to concentrate their efforts on the areas of greatest need, without having to sort through and analyze each line item of the Income Statement.

Profit and Expense Control

Weekly Position Report

1.0 INTRODUCTION

1.1 The purpose of this standard procedure is to define the method to complete the Weekly Position Report for the company.

1.2 This report is designed to provide the President with a snapshot of the business on a weekly basis.

1.3 This report is prepared and issued by the Administrative Manager every Monday morning at 10:00 A.M.

1.4 The reporting of key indicators provides the President the necessary information to have a grasp of the business conditions and to manage by exception when these indicators are outside of the acceptable parameters.

2.0 FORMAT

2.1 Bank Account

2.1.1 Show the beginning balance from all accounts from the week before. Verify the amount with the daily cash receipts. These amounts should balance.

2.1.2 Total all deposits for the week for all accounts.

2.1.3 Total all checks written.

2.1.4 Enter any adjustments either + or − into this area. Include automatic withdrawals also.

2.1.5 Add deposits, deduct checks written and +/- adjustments for "Ending Balance".

Profit and Expense Control

Weekly Position Report

2.2   Receipts

    2.2.1 Enter "Total Net Sales" for the week.

    2.2.2 Enter all money received on account.

2.3   Accounts Payable

    2.3.1 Enter Beginning Balance

    2.3.2 Total all invoices received

    2.3.3 Total all non-invoiced payables due this week.

    2.3.4 Show total of all invoices paid, including non-invoiced payables.

2.4   Line of Credit

    2.4.1 Enter "Beginning Balance"

    2.4.2 Add Deposits Made

    2.4.3 Subtract "Funds Used"

    2.4.3 Amount Available

2.5   Working Capital

    2.5.1 Enter: "Ending Balance Bank Account"

    2.5.2 Add: "Ending Balance Receipts"

    2.5.3 Add: "Ending Balance on Line of Credit"

    2.5.4 Subtract: "Ending Balance of "Accounts Payable"

    2.5.5 End Result: "Working Capital"

Profit and Expense Control

Weekly Position Report

    2.6   <u>Sales</u>

        2.6.1 Enter the Planned (Budget) or Projected Dollar Amount for each category listed at the beginning of the week.

        2.6.2 Enter the Actual Dollar Amount for each category listed at the end of the week.

        2.6.3 Compute the Variance (Difference between Planned Amount and Actual Amount).

3.0 CONCLUSION

    3.1   This one page report gives the President a great deal of information in easy readable form.

    3.2   Should something on the report not look good, then the President deals only with the section that seems out of the parameter. This is an opportunity to manage by exception.

Profit and Expense Control

<u>Executive Review</u>

Keep this list handy to remind yourself that you need to look into these areas on a daily, weekly, or monthly basis as needed by category. Get in the habit of reviewing this list daily to make sure you do not forget something and to keep controllable costs and asset control foremost in your mind.

Cash Flow

Your Administrative Manager should prepare a Cash Flow Report and have it on your desk every Monday morning by 10 A.M.

You should review this report with these questions in mind:

Are your cash needs (inflow and outflow) projected out to 6 weeks?

Does the cash flow accurately reflect the Receipt Account receipt dates?

Do the payables reflect 28 or 30 days out or more? If not are you taking advantage of discounts?

Have you received the supporting data for Receipts and Payable numbers?

Are you reacting to projected cash short falls? What is your plan?

Are you facing a short or long term crisis?

Are you using surplus wisely? Debt reduction? Investments?

Are you seeking guidance?

Receipts

Does the recap sheet reflect the current balance?

Are the records organized and verifiable?

Accounts Payable

Do the amounts paid match cash flow projections? Why not?

Are paid vendors within their terms? Spot check, prove it to yourself.

Check taxes – See where on the calendar payments are scheduled. No guesswork should be done here since penalties can be incurred.

Profit and Expense Control

Executive Review

Key Indicator Report

This report covers the critical elements of the business and should be reviewed weekly to ensure working capital is available. Your Administrative Manager completes this report after he or she collects all of the information. It also should be on your desk every Monday morning at 10:00 A.M.

Management Meeting

Was it held?

Are assignments in the Strategic Plan being completed on time?

Are new assignments being added? Strategies modified based on new facts?

Are performance reviews being conducted in all areas? Goals being met?

Are folks doing their jobs?

Does everyone understand what you want done? Does everyone know what the sale goal is for the month? Does everyone know where we are in regards to that goal this week? Are we ahead of target? What must be done to be on target or ahead?

Are you following up on problems and opportunities?

Are your direct reports giving you a status report on their goals?

Monthly P&L Statements, Budget Review and Variance Report

Are you receiving your Variance Report each month?

Are labor and other Costs of Sale in line?

Where variances exist is there a written plan of action for correction of differences between what was planned and what actually happened?

Are all your jobs profitable?

Are there any fixed costs that can be reduced or eliminated?

Quarterly Evaluations and Goal Setting

Are Performance Appraisals being held?

Are New Quarterly Goals being set?

Profit and Expense Control

Management Meetings

1.0 INTRODUCTION

1.1 The purpose of this Standard Procedure is to standardize the company's management meetings.

1.2 The basic function of a periodic meeting is to have key employees brief the President and other line managers on the status of their functional area of responsibility.

1.3 Delegating assignments, task management, information gathering and management training is a secondary function of the management meeting.

2.0 MEETING ATTENDEES

2.1 All managers and key personnel will attend management meetings as directed by the President.

2.2 The management meeting Chairperson is the President or the individual designated to chair the meeting by the President.

3.0 MANAGEMENT MEETING STRUCTURE

3.1 Periodic Management Meeting will be held in the Conference Room. Meetings will be scheduled for thirty (30) minutes and will never exceed sixty (60) minutes.

3.2 The management meeting then becomes an informal performance review tracking the day-to-day business operation.

Profit and Expense Control

Management Meetings

3.3   The agenda is given to the participants at least two (2) days in advance of the meeting. There should not be more than two or three new items.

3.4   At the meeting, old business is reviewed and reports made to update the results of previous meetings.

3.5   New business is presented and assignments made. At some meetings no new business will be discussed.

3.6   **Meeting records, activities, decisions and assignments will use a predestinated form**. The form will also be used as the meeting minutes for the record.

3.7   Special assignment and projects will use a different form to define, plan, analyze, and report each pertinent business topic to the team.

3.8   Managers will prepare an Operational Report prior to the meeting to provide an operational status report of their section and document the forecasting and planning trail. The report will provide all managers with a "thumbnail" review of the business and operational activities throughout the company.

3.9   A designated Secretary records all of the information and makes copies to give to each member affected. A copy will be kept in a meeting book for reference.

4.0   MEETING FORMAT FOR MANAGEMENTAND/OR PERIODIC MEETINGS

4.1   The meeting agenda should be prepared by the designated chairman of the meeting and circulated prior the meeting.

Profit and Expense Control

Management Meetings

4.2   Any employee who wishes to have a matter addressed will submit a written request to the Chairperson twenty-four (24) hours before the final agenda is prepared.

4.3   Meetings need to be short. Thirty minutes ideally, sixty minutes per meeting maximum.

4.4   All meetings must be agenda-driven. This means simply that all participants in the meeting will have an agenda at least two days before the meeting.

4.5   Each participant must come prepare to discuss all of the items on the agenda, even if the item is about another area. Picture how a decision on that item will impact your area and be prepared to comment. All meeting members must be proactive on all issues.

4.6   The President is the Chairman of the management meeting but this role is a role of facilitation, not domination.

4.7   A Recorder (this should rotate) will be chosen because someone must take notes. No one leaves the meeting until a person is assigned to implement or take action on a decision that has been made (only results are catalogued and not whole conversations). The Recorder catalogues all of these assignments and records the item as Old Business so it can be updated until a final progress report has been made. In order for the President to truly run the company, he must choose the method to marshal the employees behind goals and objectives.

4.8   This is called management by results – you do not just have meetings and everyone goes away and continues what they were doing previously. The primary motivation of the meeting is to ensure that action takes place that results are achieved.

Profit and Expense Control

Management Meetings

4.9   Management decision making will be delegated, as appropriate, and the responsible manager(s) will:

        4.9.1   Solve the problem, or

        4.9.2   Appoint a subordinate to study the situation and report their findings and recommendation(s).

        4.9.3   Delegate authority to an individual to recommend a course of action and set a time by which the action is to be accomplished.

        4.9.4   Discuss only the "predetermined agenda" items at the meeting.

5.0   CONCLUSION

5.1   The Periodic Meeting is a great help to the "team" if it is held in a disciplined, timely and consistent manner.

5.2   Attendees must accept the responsibility of attendance and being prepared to discuss the "announced" topics. A position report will be prepared prior to the meeting by the Office Manager.

5.3   All attendees must assist in the identification of appropriate action(s) and announcing the meeting agenda.

5.4   The meeting chairperson reviews the option(s) and recommendation(s) developed during these meetings and bases his or her decision upon the information presented.

5.5   The meeting chairperson assigns, monitors, and tracks the progress of all open and assigned "Problems, Solutions, and Projects" that have been identified.

5.6   Planned management meetings enable the factual research, intellectual evaluation and rational decision making necessary to manage and operate.

Profit and Expense Control

Management Meetings

    5.7   The President is to ensure that the team is effective. The President also must ensure that Policy is enforced and that management is meeting the established goals and objectives.

www.ingramcontent.com/pod-product-compliance
Lightning Source LLC
Chambersburg PA
CBHW050421180526
45159CB00005B/2360